# Goose b Patch ®

# The Country Friends Collection®

# Desserts

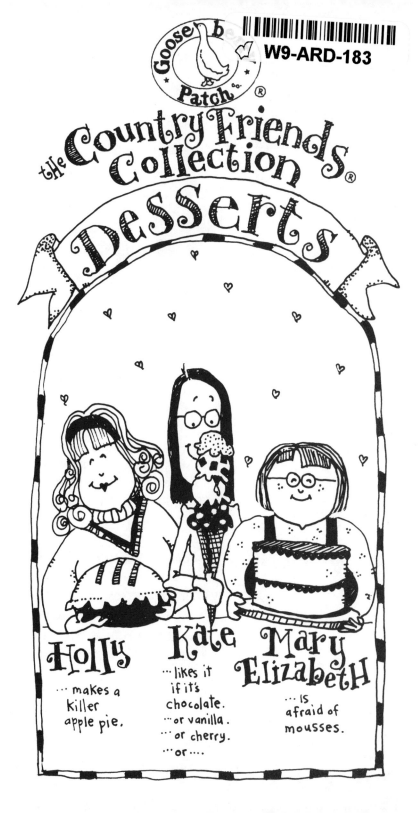

**Holly**
...makes a killer apple pie.

**Kate**
...likes it if it's chocolate.
...or vanilla.
...or cherry.
...or....

**Mary Elizabeth**
...is afraid of mousses.

# All★American Apple Pie

## INGREDIENTS

★ PASTRY FOR A DOUBLE-CRUST PIE OR TWO ALREADY-PREPARED PIE CRUSTS

★ 8-10 APPLES ~ CORED, PEELED & SLICED

★ 3 T. FLOUR

★ 1/2 to 2/3 C. SUGAR, DEPENDING ON APPLE TARTNESS

★ 1 t. CINNAMON

★ 1/4 t. NUTMEG

★ 1/8 t. GROUND ALLSPICE

★ DASH OF SALT

★ 2 T. MARGARINE

PREPARE PIE CRUST ACCORDING TO RECIPE IF MAKING FROM SCRATCH. LINE THE BOTTOM OF A 9" PIE PAN WITH ONE ROLLED PIE CRUST DOUGH. SET ASIDE.

IN A BOWL, TOSS APPLES WITH FLOUR, SUGAR, SPICES & SALT UNTIL COMPLETELY COVERED. PLACE IN PREPARED PIE SHELL AND DOT WITH MARGARINE.

BEFORE PLACING PIE'S TOP CRUST, CUT SLITS IN TOP TO VENT STEAM. PLACE CRUST ON TOP OF APPLES. TRIM EXCESS DOUGH FROM EDGES AND SEAL WITH FLUTED DESIGN. SPRINKLE CRUST WITH SUGAR.

BAKE AT 375° FOR 45-55 MINUTES.

★ TIP! TO PREVENT CRUST EDGES FROM OVER-BROWNING, COVER WITH STRIPS OF FOIL FOR FIRST HALF OF BAKING TIME.

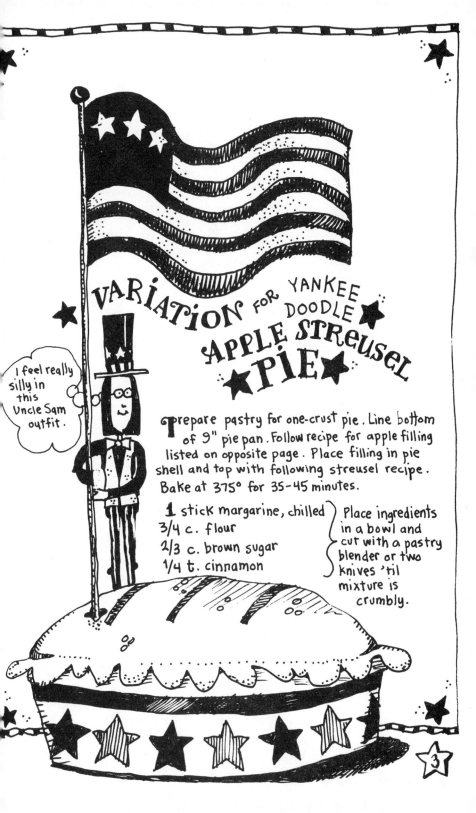

# VARIATION for YANKEE DOODLE APPLE STREUSEL ★PIE★

*I feel really silly in this Uncle Sam outfit.*

Prepare pastry for one-crust pie. Line bottom of 9" pie pan. Follow recipe for apple filling listed on opposite page. Place filling in pie shell and top with following streusel recipe. Bake at 375° for 35-45 minutes.

**1** stick margarine, chilled
3/4 c. flour
2/3 c. brown sugar
1/4 t. cinnamon

Place ingredients in a bowl and cut with a pastry blender or two knives 'til mixture is crumbly.

3

## george's favorite

# Cherry Pie

## ...UNBELIEVABLY GOOD!

### INGREDIENTS:

- PASTRY FOR A DOUBLE-CRUST PIE **or** TWO ALREADY-PREPARED PIE CRUSTS
- 1 - 1½ C. SUGAR
- 4 T. MINUTE TAPIOCA
- 4 C. PITTED TART RED CHERRIES — FRESH, FROZEN OR CANNED
- ½ t. ALMOND EXTRACT OR ½ t. CINNAMON
- 1 T. MARGARINE
- OPTIONAL: RED FOOD COLORING

**C**ombine sugar & tapioca in saucepan. Fold in fresh or frozen cherries; blend well. (If using canned cherries, drain juice from fruit and mix juice with sugar & tapioca in saucepan. Set aside cherries.)

**C**ook over medium heat, stirring constantly, 'til mixture has come to a boil. Remove from heat.

**A**dd extract & butter. (Add canned cherries at this time.) One drop of food coloring may be added to enhance color. Cool mixture before placing in pie crust shell.

**W**hile filling is cooling, prepare pie crust according to recipe if making from scratch.

**L**ine bottom of 9" pie pan with one rolled pie crust dough. Place cooled filling in pie shell. Cut slits in second pie crust and place on top of cherry filling. Seal & flute edges.

**B**ake at 400° for 30 - 35 minutes.

# DOUBLE-CRUST PASTRY

A TRADITIONAL TRIED & TRUE RECIPE!

2¼ c. FLOUR
1 t. SALT
2/3 c. SHORTENING
6 to 8 T. COLD WATER

~~~

**M**IX FLOUR & SALT IN BOWL. WITH PASTRY BLENDER OR TWO KNIVES, CUT IN SHORTENING UNTIL MIXTURE RESEMBLES SMALL PEAS OR COARSE MEAL. GENTLY MIX IN ONE TABLESPOON WATER AT A TIME 'TIL IT IS MOISTENED AND PARTICLES STICK TOGETHER. DIVIDE DOUGH INTO TWO BALLS. ROLL OUT DOUGH BETWEEN TWO SHEETS OF LIGHTLY-FLOURED WAX PAPER, FORMING A CIRCLE THAT IS ABOUT 2½" LARGER THAN DISH THAT WILL BE USED. PEEL OFF ONE SHEET OF WAX PAPER AND PLACE CRUST SIDE DOWN IN PIE PAN. GENTLY REMOVE SECOND SHEET OF WAX PAPER. REPEAT FOR TOP CRUST.

# PÂTE BRISÉE

MELT-IN-YOUR-MOUTH FRENCH PIE CRUST ~ PERFECT FOR MOIST FILLINGS!

1/2 c. COLD BUTTER
1½ c. FLOUR
1/4 t. SALT
3 to 5 T. COLD WATER

~~~

**I**N A MIXING BOWL, CUT BUTTER INTO SMALL PIECES. COMBINE FLOUR & SALT IN A FLOUR SIFTER AND SIFT INGREDIENTS OVER BUTTER IN MIXING BOWL. USING A PASTRY BLENDER OR TWO KNIVES, CUT BUTTER INTO FLOUR 'TIL MIXTURE IS COARSE. ADD ABOUT THREE TABLESPOONS OF WATER GRADUALLY TO FLOUR MIXTURE, STIRRING GENTLY WITH FORK OR KNIFE 'TIL MIXTURE IS MOIST. (ADDITIONAL WATER MAY NEED TO BE ADDED, ONE TABLESPOON AT A TIME.) DOUGH SHOULD FORM A SOFT BALL AND NOT STICK TO FINGERS. WRAP DOUGH IN WAX PAPER AND REFRIGERATE FOR ONE HOUR BEFORE USING. (REFRIGERATING HELPS REDUCE SHRINKAGE AND MAKES A MORE TENDER CRUST.)

# APPLE DUMPLINGS

AN EXCELLENT
FALL DESSERT
WHEN
APPLES ARE AT
THEIR PEAK

# INGREDIENTS:

PASTRY FOR DOUBLE-CRUST PIE
6 SMALL BAKING APPLES,
       PEELED & CORED
6 T. SUGAR
½ t. CINNAMON

¼ t. NUTMEG
⅛ t. ALLSPICE
3 T. RAISINS - optional
3 T. CHOPPED PECANS
    OR WALNUTS - optional

# HOW TO:

PREPARE PASTRY. ROLL PASTRY INTO A 21"x14" RECTANGLE ON A FLOURED SURFACE. CUT PASTRY INTO SIX 7" SQUARES.

PLACE ONE APPLE IN CENTER OF EACH PASTRY SQUARE. IN A SMALL BOWL, COMBINE SUGAR & SPICES. SPRINKLE SUGAR & SPICE MIX OVER APPLES. FILL CENTER OF APPLES WITH RAISINS & NUTS IF YOU WISH. BRING UP CORNERS OF PASTRY, COVERING APPLES; PRESS EDGES TOGETHER TO SEAL.

PLACE DUMPLINGS IN 13"x9" BAKING DISH OR SIX INDIVIDUAL OVEN-PROOF DISHES.

IN A SAUCEPAN, MAKE A BATCH OF

## CINNAMON SPICE SAUCE

| | |
|---|---|
| 3/4 C. BROWN SUGAR | 1/4 t. CINNAMON |
| 1/4 C. HONEY | 1/8 t. NUTMEG |
| 1/2 C. WATER | 3 T. BUTTER OR MARGARINE |

COMBINE SUGAR, HONEY, WATER & SPICES. BRING MIXTURE TO A BOIL & STIR IN BUTTER. POUR MIXTURE OVER DUMPLINGS. BAKE AT 400° FOR 35 TO 40 MINUTES OR UNTIL CRUST IS GOLDEN BROWN AND APPLES ARE TENDER. SERVE WARM WITH CREAM.

# MARY ELIZABETH'S FABULOUS

## Fruit Crisp

- **4-5** c. fruit (choose from sliced apples, peaches, cherries, blueberries or diced rhubarb)
- **1/4** c. sugar
- **3-4** T. water
- **1/2** t. cinnamon
- **1/8** t. nutmeg (great with peaches)
- **1/8** t. allspice (tasty with apples)
- **1** t. lemon juice (1 t. grated orange peel with rhubarb)

Combine ingredients in a greased baking dish. If using canned fruit, drain juice before mixing with ingredients.
Cherries & rhubarb may require at least two to three times more sugar.

Make topping — recipe on next page! ⭐ 8

# FABULOUS FRUIT CRISP TOPPING RECIPE:

xxxxxxxxxxxxxxxxxxxxxxxxxxxxxxxxxxxxxxxxx

- 1 c. rolled oats
- 1/2 c. brown sugar
- 3 T. sugar
- 1/2 c. flour
- 1/4 c. wheat germ
- 1/2 t. cinnamon
- 1/4 c. chopped pecans or walnuts
- 8 T. butter or margarine, cut in cubes

Mix together 'til coarse & crumbly. Sprinkle topping over fruit filling. Bake at 350° for 30 to 40 minutes until top is crisp golden brown and fruit is bubbly.

## MARY ELIZABETH'S KITCHEN NOTES

**Cobbler:** a deep dish dessert of fruit filling topped with a biscuit dough crust. The dough is dropped in heaping mounds on the filling or cut into round shapes and overlapped over the fruit.

**Crisp:** fruit filling covered with a crisp, crunchy mixture of flour, butter, brown sugar & nuts.

**Brown Betty:** an old-fashioned dessert in which a crumb mixture is layered between fruit layers. ★ Wonder where the name came from?

**Pandowdy:** "Dowdying" means to break up the pastry crust with a spoon and push the pieces back into the fruit filling. Usually done near end of baking time or just before serving.

♥ HAPPY HOME RECIPE ♥

4 c. love
2 c. loyalty
3 c. forgiveness
1 c. friendship
1 c. kindness
6 spoons understanding

5 spoons hope
2 spoons tenderness
4 qt. faith
1 barrel of laughter
ray of sunshine

Take love & loyalty, mix thoroughly with faith. Blend it with tenderness, kindness, understanding & forgiveness. Add friendship & hope, sprinkle abundantly with laughter. Bake it with sunshine. Serve daily in generous helpings.
— Author unknown

The World is so full of a number of things, I'm sure we should all be as happy as Kings. - Robert Louis Stevenson

9

# Holly's Chocolate Silk Pie

## The rich filling is as smooth as silk!

unbaked pastry shell
3/4 c. brown sugar
1/4 c. margarine or butter, softened
3 eggs
1 1/4 c. semi-sweet chocolate chips, melted

1 1/2 t. instant coffee
1 t. almond extract
1 c. toasted almonds, chopped
1/4 c. flour
1/2 c. whole almonds

In a mixing bowl, beat brown sugar & margarine until fluffy. Beat in one egg at a time. Mix in chocolate, coffee & almond extract. Add chopped almonds and flour; mix well. Pour filling into unbaked pie shell. Decorate top with whole almonds. Bake on lower rack in oven 25 minutes at 375°. Cool. Chill pie at least one hour before serving.

# Mary Elizabeth's Guide to Perfect Pie Crusts

Remember...
## Less is Best.

(Don't look that way at me. I'm not talking about **EATING** the pie — I'm talking about **MAKING** it.)

**T**ough pie crusts are the result of too much flour, too much mixing, too much rough handling. So — be tender, and remember that less is always better when dealing with dough.

**T**oo much water makes crust soggy. It won't stand up to juices in fruit fillings, and you'll have a sloppy mess at serving time. You're not filling a swimming pool — you're making pie crust, so add water <u>one</u> tablespoon at a time... And make the water very cold.

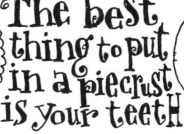

## The best thing to put in a piecrust is your teeth.

# Good apple pies are a considerable part of our domestic happiness.
~ Jane Austen

# southern Peach Cobbler

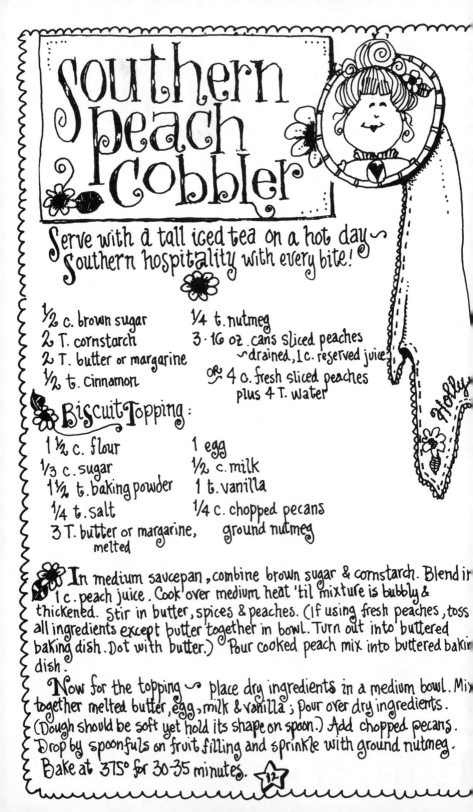

*Serve with a tall iced tea on a hot day ~ Southern hospitality with every bite!*

½ c. brown sugar
2 T. cornstarch
2 T. butter or margarine
½ t. cinnamon

¼ t. nutmeg
3 · 16 oz. cans sliced peaches
 ~ drained, 1 c. reserved juice
OR 4 c. fresh sliced peaches
 plus 4 T. water

## Biscuit Topping:

1½ c. flour
⅓ c. sugar
1½ t. baking powder
¼ t. salt
3 T. butter or margarine, melted

1 egg
½ c. milk
1 t. vanilla
¼ c. chopped pecans
 ground nutmeg

In medium saucepan, combine brown sugar & cornstarch. Blend in 1 c. peach juice. Cook over medium heat 'til mixture is bubbly & thickened. Stir in butter, spices & peaches. (If using fresh peaches, toss all ingredients except butter together in bowl. Turn out into buttered baking dish. Dot with butter.) Pour cooked peach mix into buttered baking dish.

Now for the topping ~ place dry ingredients in a medium bowl. Mix together melted butter, egg, milk & vanilla; pour over dry ingredients. (Dough should be soft yet hold its shape on spoon.) Add chopped pecans. Drop by spoonfuls on fruit filling and sprinkle with ground nutmeg. Bake at 375° for 30-35 minutes.

Lay out the Welcome Mat...

...invite friends in for coffee & dessert. No meal to fuss over, so you're free to visit.

Keep it Simple ~ dress it up! Desserts look beautiful served on a clear glass plate with a white paper doily underneath... easy & elegant.

Most of all ~ enjoy your guests ~ Eat, Drink, and Be Merry, For Tomorrow We Diet.

The ripest peach is highest on the tree. - James Whitcomb Riley

# Kate's Cooking Lesson

# Granny's Gingerbread with Lemon Sauce

¼ c. sugar
¼ c. butter or margarine
1 egg
½ c. light molasses
1 c. flour
½ t. baking powder
¼ t. baking soda

¼ t. salt
½ t. ginger
½ t. cinnamon
⅛ t. allspice
⅛ t. cloves
6 T. warm water

**Ok, Kate** — get all the ingredients out first. Preheat the oven, and we'll begin! See — this isn't so hard, is it?

*I think it's hopeless.*

*forget about it, Grandma.*

*I think it's hopeless.*

**N**ow... <u>cream the butter & sugar together</u> in a medium-size bowl. Ooops — that's all right. We have other mixing bowls. Did you cut yourself? *oh dear*

**N**ext, we <u>add the egg & molasses</u>. Honey, you have to crack the egg first. Yes, just like that. Now just pick out all those little bits of shell.... <u>Beat it well now.</u> *oh my*

**Y**ou're doing fine, dear. Just relax. **C**ombine the flour, baking powder, baking soda & spices together in a bowl. **O**K! Good!

**N**ow, <u>alternating with water</u>, <u>gradually add the dry ingredients to the creamed mixture.</u> KATE!! I SAID "GRADUALLY!" *my goodness*

**P**our the batter in a greased 8" x 8" pan. That's the one, yes. We'll <u>bake it for 35 or 45 minutes at 350°</u> or 'til it passes the toothpick test. **N**o, don't leave the hotpad inside the oven with the pan... grab that fire extinguisher and we'll have that out in a jiffy. Why don't you go out in the yard and read? *please Lord*

**I**'ll whip up the **lemon sauce** this time. You stand over there on the other side of the room and don't touch anything. You can help me next time, alright?

- 3/4 c. sugar
- 1 1/2 t. cornstarch
- 1 c. water
- 1/2 c. apple cider or juice
- 5 T. lemon juice
- 1 T. butter
- 1/2 t. lemon zest, finely grated
- dash of salt

In a saucepan, combine sugar, cornstarch, cider & water. Stir constantly over medium heat — bring to boil. Reduce heat to low & simmer. Stir until thickened & clear. Remove from stove & stir in lemon juice, butter, zest & salt. Serve warm over gingerbread. Isn't that Good? **I couldn't have done it without you, Kate!**

# QUICK UPSIDE·DOWN CAKE

YELLOW CAKE MIX

RINGS

## Topping:

3 T. BUTTER
1 CAN PINEAPPLE RINGS*,
   DRAINED ~ RESERVE 2 T. JUICE
1/3 c. BROWN SUGAR

1/2 c. NUTS, CHOPPED (OPTIONAL)
MARASCHINO CHERRIES,
     HALVED

MELT BUTTER IN 9" CAKE PAN. STIR IN BROWN SUGAR, RESERVED JUICE & NUTS. LAY PINEAPPLE RINGS WITH A MARASCHINO CHERRY HALF IN CENTER ON TOP OF BROWN SUGAR MIXTURE. SET ASIDE.

*SUBSTITUTE FRESH CHUNKS OF RHUBARB, APRICOT HALVES, SLICED PEACHES OR PLUMS FOR PINEAPPLE RINGS FOR A REFRESHING, CREATIVE TWIST!

..So good & quick, you'll feel a bit guilty about accepting all the applaus

## Cake:

3/4 c. SUGAR  
2 EGGS, beaten  
1 t. VANILLA  

1½ t. BAKING POWDER  
1½ c. FLOUR  
¼ t. SALT  

1/3 c. butter  
1/2 c. MILK  

SIFT BAKING POWDER, FLOUR & SALT TOGETHER. SET ASIDE. CREAM BUTTER & SUGAR. BEAT IN EGGS, VANILLA & MILK. ON LOW SPEED, SLOWLY ADD FLOUR TO CREAMED MIXTURE. MIX WELL. POUR BATTER OVER FRUIT TOPPING. BAKE AT 350° FOR 30 TO 40 MINUTES. LET COOL 5 MINUTES IN PAN. INVERT ONTO AN OVEN-PROOF PLATE. SERVE WARM WITH DOLLOPS OF WHIPPED CREAM.

**Quick Tip!** COMPANY COMING **NOW?** MIX UP A BOXED ONE-LAYER WHITE OR YELLOW CAKE MIX & POUR OVER FRUIT TOPPING.

# "Never hurry and Never Worry."

—E.B. WHITE  
(Charlotte's advice to Wilbur in Charlotte's Web)

## Sweetened Whipped Cream:

1 c. whipping cream, chilled  
¼ c. powdered sugar  
1 t. vanilla  

Combine all ingredients in chilled bowl. Whip 'til stiff peaks are formed. (Don't overmix! It can turn to butter very quickly.) Chill.

## Bring on the Dessert!

# STUFFED BAKED APPLES
## WITH RICH & YUMMY CARAMEL SAUCE

**For one apple:**

- 1 to 2 t. walnuts or pecans, chopped
- 2 T. brown sugar
- 1 t. butter
- 1/8 t. cinnamon
- dash nutmeg
- 1 T. granola
- baking apple such as Rome Beauty, Winesap or Golden Delicious

Remove core & peel from upper half of apple. Place in oven-proof baking dish. Combine nuts, brown sugar, butter & spices; place in cored center of apple. Top with granola. Place about 1 T. water around apple in dish. Bake at 350° for 30-40 minutes. Serve warm with Rich Caramel Sauce.

## SAUCE:

- 3 t. cornstarch
- 1/2 c. cold water
- 3 T. honey
- 6 T. butter or margarine
- 6 T. brown sugar
- dash of cinnamon & nutmeg

Blend cornstarch & cold water in saucepan 'til smooth. Add the remaining ingredients to saucepan. Stir constantly ~ heat until it's thickened & boiling. Remove from heat and serve warm.

A wonderful way to end an Autumn dinner!

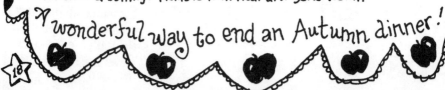

♪ Shoo-fly pie and Apple pan-dowdy,
makes your eyes light up
and your stomach say howdy!
~OLD SONG~

# HOWDY PEAR PANDOWDY

## Serve warm with cream or ice cream!

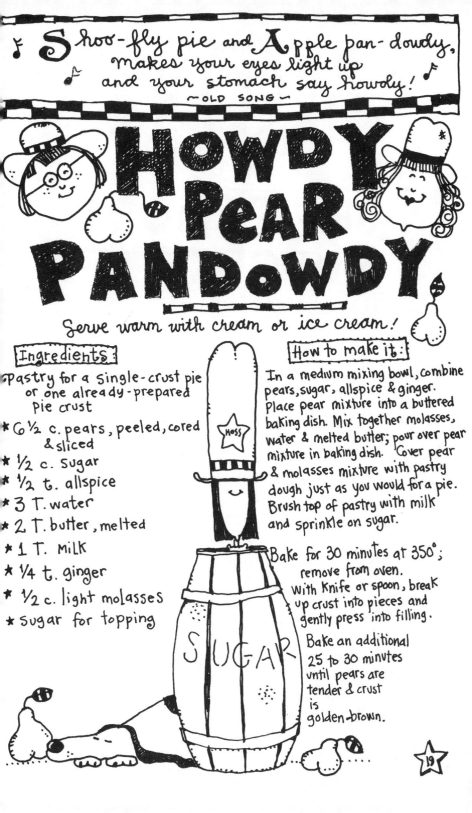

### Ingredients :

- Pastry for a single-crust pie or one already-prepared pie crust
- ★ 6½ c. pears, peeled, cored & sliced
- ★ ½ c. sugar
- ★ ½ t. allspice
- ★ 3 T. water
- ★ 2 T. butter, melted
- ★ 1 T. milk
- ★ ¼ t. ginger
- ★ ½ c. light molasses
- ★ sugar for topping

### How to make it :

In a medium mixing bowl, combine pears, sugar, allspice & ginger. Place pear mixture into a buttered baking dish. Mix together molasses, water & melted butter; pour over pear mixture in baking dish. Cover pear & molasses mixture with pastry dough just as you would for a pie. Brush top of pastry with milk and sprinkle on sugar.

Bake for 30 minutes at 350°; remove from oven. With knife or spoon, break up crust into pieces and gently press into filling.

Bake an additional 25 to 30 minutes until pears are tender & crust is golden-brown.

# Lead me Not into Temptation.

## TRIPLE DELIGHT FUDGE CAKE

### A CHOCOLATE LOVER'S DREAM!

COCOA
DEEP CHOCOLATE OR FUDGE CAKE MIX
3½ OZ. PKG. CHOCOLATE FUDGE INSTANT PUDDING MIX

¼ C. OIL, ONLY IF MIX CALLS FOR OIL

3 TO 4 EGGS
1/4 C. MAYONNAISE
WATER ~ AMOUNT ON CAKE MIX

**G**REASE 3. 8" ROUND LAYER PANS AND DUST WITH COCOA. COMBINE INGREDIENTS IN A MIXING BOWL ~ BEAT FOR ABOUT 2 MINUTES. POUR INTO PANS. BAKE ACCORDING TO PACKAGE INSTRUCTIONS, ABOUT 30 MINUTES OR UNTIL TOOTHPICK INSERTED IN CAKE'S CENTER COMES OUT CLEAN. COOL IN PANS 5 MINUTES, THEN INVERT AND COOL ON RACKS.

## MOUSSE FILLING:

3½ OZ. PKG. CHOCOLATE FUDGE INSTANT PUDDING
1 TO 1¼ C. MILK
3/4 C. WHIPPED TOPPING
1 T. INSTANT COFFEE OR 2 T. KAHLUA

**M**IX PUDDING & MILK TOGETHER. FOLD IN WHIPPED TOPPING AND COFFEE OR KAHLUA. CHILL.

I will be strong, I will be strong...

20

# TO ASSEMBLE CAKE:

PLACE 1 LAYER ON A CAKE PLATE AND SPREAD A LAYER OF MOUSSE ON TOP. TOP WITH 2ND CAKE LAYER. AGAIN, SPREAD WITH MOUSSE. TOP WITH FINAL CAKE LAYER. FOR A REALLY ELEGANT 6-LAYER CAKE, SPLIT CAKE LAYERS AND FILL WITH MOUSSE AS WELL. KEEP WELL CHILLED.

ABOUT AN HOUR BEFORE SERVING, TOP CAKE WITH GLAZE.

Well, maybe just a teensy little slice...

# GLAZE:

1 c. SEMI-SWEET CHOCOLATE CHIPS
1/2 c. MILK CHOCOLATE CHIPS
3 t. BUTTER

4½ t. MILK
4½ t. LIGHT CORN SYRUP

COMBINE INGREDIENTS IN MICROWAVE DISH. HEAT FOR 30 SECONDS ON MEDIUM POWER. STIR. HEAT AN ADDITIONAL 30 SECONDS. STIR. CONTINUE 'TIL CHIPS ARE COMPLETELY MELTED AND GLAZE IS SMOOTH & GLOSSY. SPREAD OVER TOP AND LET DRIP DOWN SIDES OF CAKE. (IF IT SEEMS TOO THICK, HEAT & ADD LITTLE MORE MILK, NEVER WATER.)

GIVE ME THE WHOLE CAKE NOW AND NOBODY GETS HURT.

I doubt whether the world holds for anyone a more soul-stirring surprise than the first adventure with ice cream. ~Heywood Broun

## HOMEMADE VANILLA ice cream

★ COOL, RICH & CREAMY!

4 EGGS
2½ c. SUGAR
6 c. MILK
4 c. HEAVY CREAM
1½ T. VANILLA
½ t. SALT

★

Add sugar gradually to beaten eggs, beating well after each addition. When mixture is becoming very stiff, add remaining ingredients & mix thoroughly. Pour into gallon ice cream freezer & follow the manufacturer's directions for freezing.

PUT A SPARKLER IN THE TOP OF A MOUNTAIN OF ICE CREAM FOR A DESSERT NOT-SOON-FORGOTTEN!

"HUNGER IS THE BEST SAUCE IN THE WORLD." ~Cervantes, "Don Quixote"

# FANTASTIC FUDGE SAUCE

A QUICK & EASY TOPPER YOU CAN MAKE ON THE STOVE OR IN THE MICRO-WAVE!

2/3 C. EVAPORATED MILK

6 OZ. PKG. SEMI-SWEET CHOCOLATE CHIPS

1 C. MARSHMALLOW CREME

* * *

Combine milk & chocolate chips. Cook over low heat until chips are melted completely. Stir in marshmallow creme until well-blended. Serve over ice cream.

★ HINT! Use over cake or as a dipping sauce for fruit...

*delicious!*

# ice cream ideas

**D**ip vanilla in ball-shapes out on a chilled cookie sheet. Roll in coconut and sprinkle with crystal-clear ice-cream jimmies... a pretty dessert at Christmastime served with thin slices of chocolate cake, or a refreshing "SNOWBALL" during the hottest afternoons in August.

**S**erve homemade ice cream in plastic sand buckets ∽ use the shovel, too!

**H**ave a SUNDAE afternoon: invite friends over ∽ each one brings a different flavor of ice cream and a special topping ∽ and spend a happy (and fattening) hour or two experimenting.

## KATE'S COLUMN
### FOR THE
### CULINARILY DIS-INCLINED

Dear Kate:
We have a very good friend who is an absolute disaster in the kitchen. She breaks things, she burns things, she just can't follow a recipe! Do you have any suggestions for her that might help? She's entertaining soon. Signed, ~~Polly~~ & ~~Mary Ellen~~ anonymous

... ★ ...

Dear Anonymous : Tell your friend to serve ice cream cones to her guests. Any klutz can do it, and everybody likes 'em.
(P.S. Do I know this person?)

23

# Mary Elizabeth's Luscious Lemon pudding cake

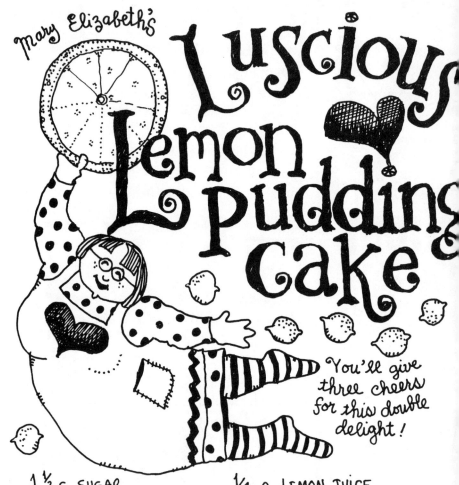

*You'll give three cheers for this double delight!*

1½ c. SUGAR
6 T. ALL-PURPOSE FLOUR
¼ t. SALT
6 T. BUTTER ~ MELTED

¼ c. LEMON JUICE
2 t. LEMON ZEST ~ FINELY GRATED
4 EGGS ~ SEPARATED
1½ c. MILK

IN A LARGE MIXING BOWL, COMBINE SUGAR, FLOUR & SALT. IN A SEPARATE BOWL, BEAT TOGETHER BUTTER, LEMON JUICE, LEMON ZEST, EGG YOLKS & MILK. POUR OVER DRY INGREDIENTS ~ MIX WELL. BEAT EGG WHITES 'TIL STIFF PEAKS FORM. GENTLY FOLD STIFFENED EGG WHITES INTO LEMON MIXTURE. POUR BATTER INTO A BUTTERED 8" X 8" BAKING DISH. PLACE THE DISH IN A LARGER PAN & PLACE ON MIDDLE RACK IN OVEN. POUR HOT WATER INTO LARGER PAN 'TIL IT REACHES HALFWAY UP SIDES OF BAKING DISH. BAKE 40-45 MINUTES AT 350°, OR 'TIL SURFACE IS GOLDEN AND SPRINGS UP AT LIGHT TOUCH. SERVE WARM OR CHILLED.

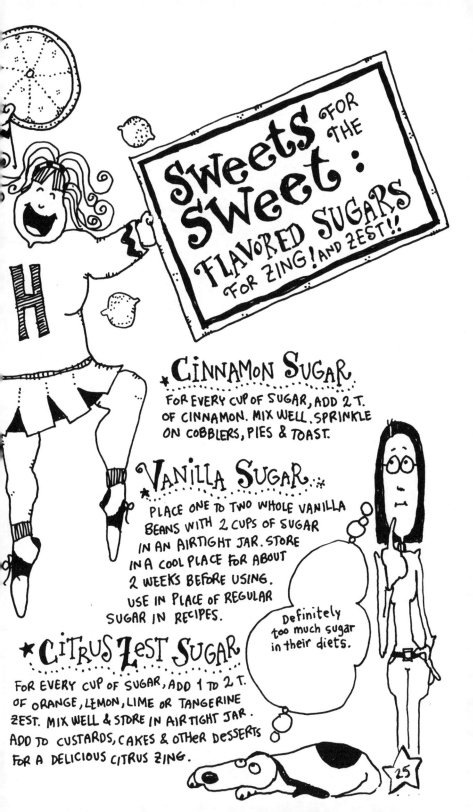

# Sweets for the Sweet: FLAVORED SUGARS for Zing! and Zest!!

## ★ Cinnamon Sugar

For every cup of sugar, add 2 T. of cinnamon. Mix well. Sprinkle on cobblers, pies & toast.

## ★ Vanilla Sugar ★

Place one to two whole vanilla beans with 2 cups of sugar in an airtight jar. Store in a cool place for about 2 weeks before using. Use in place of regular sugar in recipes.

## ★ Citrus Zest Sugar

For every cup of sugar, add 1 to 2 T. of orange, lemon, lime or tangerine zest. Mix well & store in airtight jar. Add to custards, cakes & other desserts for a delicious citrus zing.

Definitely too much sugar in their diets.

25

OOOOOO·LA·LA·!

# French Bread Pudding

*A soul-satisfying treat the whole family will love!*

## INGREDIENTS:

5 c. cinnamon, French or rich egg bread, crust trimmed & cut into cubes
3 T. butter, melted
2½ c. milk
½ c. whipping cream
4 eggs
½ c. sugar
1½ t. vanilla

½ t. cinnamon, or to taste if using plain bread
½ t. nutmeg
1 t. orange zest, finely grated (optional)
⅛ t. salt
confectioner's sugar

Butter a deep casserole or baking dish and fill with bread cubes. Drizzle melted butter over bread cubes. Whisk together milk, cream, eggs, sugar, vanilla, cinnamon, nutmeg, orange zest & salt in a medium mixing bowl 'til well blended. Pour over bread. Place baking dish in a large pan and place in oven. Fill larger pan with hot water until it reaches 'halfway' up the sides of the baking dish. Bake at 350° for 45-50 minutes or until knife inserted in center comes out clean. Before serving, sprinkle with confectioner's sugar. Serve warm or chilled.

Mmmm.

The proof of the pudding is in the eating.

-Cervantes

# Ain't Life Grand!

Just think of Life's little pleasures ~ all the simple things we love! A good share of them seem to fall into the dessert category ~ work (eat!) your way thru our list:

★ a ROOT BEER float in a frosty mug

★ plain old CHOCOLATE pudding served in a very fancy champagne glass

★ ORANGE POPSICLES on a hot summer day

★ CHOCOLATE CHIP COOKIE DOUGH!

★ Roasted marshmallows over the fireplace - the gooier the better

★ frozen BANANA SLICES

★ animal crackers right outta the box

★ JELLY BEANS

27

Perfect with the fresh
sweet fruits of
Summer...

# Summer

# Shortcake

2 c. flour
2 t. baking powder
1/3 c. sugar
1/4 t. salt
6 T. butter
2/3 c. milk
1 egg, beaten
1 t. vanilla
Sugar for topping
fresh fruit, cut up
   & sprinkled with
   sugar

In a mixing bowl, combine flour, baking powder, sugar & salt. Cut in butter with a pastry blender 'til mixture is coarse. Add milk, egg & vanilla. Mix well. Drop by spoonfuls onto greased sheet or roll out on lightly floured surface ~ cut shapes with cookie cutters. Sprinkle tops with sugar. Bake at 400° for 12 to 15 minutes or 'til golden brown. Split warm cake ~ fill with fruit and top with more fruit and whipped cream (recipe on page 17)

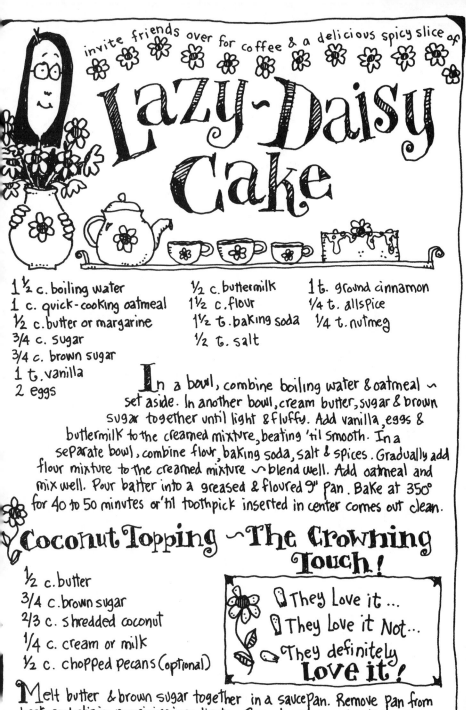

# Lazy~Daisy Cake

invite friends over for coffee & a delicious spicy slice of

1½ c. boiling water
1 c. quick-cooking oatmeal
½ c. butter or margarine
3/4 c. sugar
3/4 c. brown sugar
1 t. vanilla
2 eggs

½ c. buttermilk
1½ c. flour
1½ t. baking soda
½ t. salt

1 t. ground cinnamon
1/4 t. allspice
1/4 t. nutmeg

**I**n a bowl, combine boiling water & oatmeal ~ set aside. In another bowl, cream butter, sugar & brown sugar together until light & fluffy. Add vanilla, eggs & buttermilk to the creamed mixture, beating 'til smooth. In a separate bowl, combine flour, baking soda, salt & spices. Gradually add flour mixture to the creamed mixture ~ blend well. Add oatmeal and mix well. Pour batter into a greased & floured 9" pan. Bake at 350° for 40 to 50 minutes or 'til toothpick inserted in center comes out clean.

## Coconut Topping ~ The Crowning Touch!

½ c. butter
3/4 c. brown sugar
2/3 c. shredded coconut
1/4 c. cream or milk
½ c. chopped pecans (optional)

They Love it...
They Love it Not...
They definitely **Love it!**

**M**elt butter & brown sugar together in a saucepan. Remove pan from heat and stir in remaining ingredients. Spread over top of baked cake. Place under broiler until topping is bubbly & golden. (Be careful not to burn it!) Cool completely before serving.

peaches. cherries.

Great for a Kids' Party! Serve slices on plastic FRISBEES to each child. WHAT FUN!

Grapes · apple slices · strawberries · bananas · kiwi · bananas ·

# F·A·N·C·Y
# FRUIT PIZZA

OUR KIDS LOVE TO FIX (AND EAT) THIS SUMMERTIME TREA

**1** ROLL REFRIGERATED SUGAR COOKIE DOUGH

**3** OZ. PKG. CREAM CHEESE, SOFTENED

**1/3** C. BROWN SUGAR

**1** C. SOUR CREAM

**1/2** t. VANILLA

**4** C. ASSORTED FRESH FRUIT, SLICED

**1/3** C. APPLE OR CURRANT JELL MELTED (OPTIONAL

To FORM CRUST, PRESS COOKIE DOUGH INTO 12" PIZZA PAN. BAKE AT 350° F 10-15 MINUTES OR 'TIL GOLDEN BROWN. COOL. BEAT TOGETHER CREAM CHEESE BROWN SUGAR, SOUR CREAM & VANILLA. SPREAD ON COOLED COOKIE CRUST. NOW ARRANGE SLICED FRUIT ON TOP. BRUSH MELTED JELLY OVER TOP OF FRUIT I YOU WISH.

REFRIGERATE 'TIL SERVED.

# Genuine truly ★ old ★ fashioned Pound Cake

really truly

very good

3 c. flour
1 t. baking powder
½ t. nutmeg
¼ t. salt
1½ c. butter

3 c. powdered sugar
2 t. vanilla
5 eggs
¾ c. half & half

**G**rease and coat with granulated sugar two 8" loaf pans or a 10" fluted tube pan.

**I**n a bowl, combine flour, baking powder, nutmeg & salt. Set aside.

**C**ream together butter, powdered sugar & vanilla.

**A**dd eggs one at a time, beating well after each addition. Mixture should be light & fluffy.

**M**ix in half of flour mixture until smooth. **B**lend in half & half. Beat in remaining dry ingredients until smooth.

**P**our cake batter into pans. **B**ake at 350° for 45 to 75 minutes (depending on pan size) or until a wooden pick inserted in center comes out clean. Cool in pan about 10 minutes before removing.

**Y**UMMY VARIATION: MAKE IT A CHOCOLATE CHIP POUND CAKE BY DELETING NUTMEG AND ADDING ¼ c. MINI SEMI-SWEET CHOCOLATE CHIPS!

## Dessert Collection Index

# "Follow Your Bliss."

— Joseph Campbell